While Bethlehem Sleeps

By Penny J. Johnson

To my parents, Paul and Pam Olson.

Table of Contents

Acknowledgements

Unless otherwise noted or quoted, many of these poems are inspired by the biblical narrative and characters found in Gospel of Luke.

The poems entitled "Warmed Memories," the excerpt from "Snow," "His Mother's Joy," "On Watching a Church Choir One Sunday," and "Make Me Believe in Christmas" appear in *The Last Time We Were Children* published by Tate Publishing and Enterprises in 2007.

Many thanks to the following:

Melissa Howard for her insight as a reader, poet, and friend.

Matthew C. Merten for his expertise in designing the cover.

My church families who requested my skills as a poet and editor for Advent readings and in-house publications.

Anne M. Nymann, my grandmother, who preceded me in the tradition of writing Christmas card poems for my mother.

Pam Olson, my mother, whose annual Christmas card request produced many of these poems.

Paul Olson, my father, who provided the incentive to publish a paperback version for use as a ministry tool.

Dave who encouraged me to think beyond traditional publishing and to share my words with others.

Nate, Jarrod, and Marcus who bless me with their smiles and hugs.

Jesus Christ, the First Gift, who is the reason for every season.

Hope

Humbled faces pressed to dust

Opened palms reaching, seeking to receive

Prophesy, understanding, speech

Enough to describe visions to blind eyes.

On the Day God Created Trees,

The moment seeds took root

For a tree with fruit forsaken

Beside one named after life,

He marked along the path foreknown

The boughs for the Newborn's corn-crib

Not far from the cross-beams of rebirth.

While Bethlehem Sleeps

a priest dictates from the Torah

to his son at bedtime.

When he finishes, the boy, stifling a yawn,

cries out,

Tell me a new story, Abba.

Swallowing hard, clearing his throat, the priest tells

of an old man with a barren wife

visited by an angel who said...

Abba, I've heard this one!
It's Abraham.

... the boy will have the Spirit from birth,

should not drink wine or fermented drink...

Then it's Samson.

The old man did not believe God's angel

who said a child would be born to him...

It can't be Elijah! He didn't have a son.

...so the man could not speak until

after writing the name on a tablet....

Moses wrote on tablets!

Then his mouth opened....

Whose mouth opened?

The priest smiles at his son

whose words already drip like wild honey

whose thoughts jump like locusts in the grass.

Someday, John, you will know.

Wishes

I wish to hold Shakespeare's pen,
        to write sonnets all day long

for people to memorize for centuries.

I wish to sit on Christ's lap

and feel the love I imagine He has for me.

I wish to be like the man whose child was possessed,

and have just enough faith, ask for a bit more.

I wish children would wake

as quietly as they sleep.

I wish my words always came out like lullabies

and never like machine gun fire.

I wish to tell my grandfather all the things he's missed,

ask him if he knows more answers in heaven.

Like him, I wish I appreciated all the moments,
the ones I miss

when I wish for things to be
the way I wish for them to be.

While Bethlehem Sleeps

Anna never leaves

yet never fully enters

the temple's inner sanctum

but she knows

one day grace

will split the divide

allowing access

to those willing

to stay.

The Commander and the Prophet[i]

The prophet claims to see the future,

But he won't come out to see me!

He doesn't even wave a hand

over my twisted, useless ones!

He tells me to dip myself in the Jordan.

Why that river? Why not any?

Seven times, he says.

Why seven? Why not seventy?

But, my servants say, he is a prophet.

Why not listen? Why not hope?

So, I go and immerse my unclean body.

All the while wondering, why hope?

But, my wasted skin comes up restored!

My stony heart leaves me!

I send a gift of gratitude to the prophet,

but he refuses.

He says he serves the Lord.

From now on, so do I.

Prayer: Praise You, Lord, for giving hope in hopeless situations! You alone can heal the diseases of our body. You alone soften our hardened hearts. May we obey Your commands, so that our hope in You remains constant. In Your unending hope, we pray, Amen.

Peace

Plumage unfurled in flight, the dove

Explores the skies, the deeps, the land;

Alights on an olive vine's foliage;

Cradles a branch in his firm-footed grasp;

Extends it toward the Child's uplifted hand.

While Bethlehem Sleeps

a king tosses in his bed,

pulling covers over his head

wondering how long

 until dawn

eclipses the starlight shining

in his eyes.

Trust

Tumultuous tasks

Ruin respite

Until unbidden

Solace, serenity

Temper trepidation.

Cookie Days

Today has been a cookie day.

I looked at my schedule

like refrigerator-hard butter,

but it softened by mid-day

into the pliable cream of quiet,

that sweet-sugar stillness with egg-yellow sunlight

when even flour clouds thicken life's battered
        runniness.

If stress like oven's heat causes cracks

it reveals doneness, the short tempered buzzer
        turned off,

somehow producing a multitude of
        delectable memories

to savor, to melt the mouth, and make it smile.

Christmas Wonder

Do we strain to hear above the roaring winds

as we travel down snowy paths,
        our sleigh runners sliding,

our horsepower exerting its own rhythm

as bells jingle throughout our mingled journeys?

As we travel down snowy paths,
        our sleigh runners slide

through our memories--shimmering, silver

bells jingling throughout our mingled journeys

with a canon of carols dangling in the air
        like ornaments on a fresh-cut tree.

Our memories, shimmering and silver,

forget with all the lists of gifts

with the canons of carols. Dangling in the air
        like ornaments on a fresh-cut tree,

we cannot see the star.

We cannot see the Star

with our horsepower exerting its own rhythm.

Forget all the lists of gifts.

Strain to hear above the roaring winds.

Stained Glass

An image of stained glass

projected on a screen—

certainly not the same as cathedral

windows, light reflected,

colors on faces, illuminated

piece by piece.

I want to see the real thing—

cherubim flying above the manger

the mother of God and designated father

wearing halos, glowing by spirit,

marveling at the baby, incarnate king—

I want to be the real thing, too.

Like a cathedral

window, light reflected,

his color on my face, illuminated

piece by piece.

While Bethlehem Sleeps

Shepherds counting sheep

fight the urge to sleep

when sudden angelic light

momentarily blinds their sight

when more voices than the stars

blare in their ears like an urgent alarm

"Glory to God in the highest, and on earth peace

among men with whom He is pleased,"[ii]

one angel spreads words like protective wings

over startled fledglings and gently sings

"Do not fear!"

Then in a whisper only they can hear

tells them the signs

to follow and find

a cloth-wrapped child named

"God saves," a gift for them to claim.

The God-Wrestler[iii]

I am a born-fighter.

I am a God-wrestler.

Last night, I fought God face to face.

He could have taken anything.

He could have killed me.

Instead He gave me reminders—

a limp for life

and a new name—

because I struggled with God and men

and have overcome.

But, now Esau comes.

This born-fighter is afraid.

Esau's face is like the face of God.

He has the right to take anything,

the right to kill us all.

He doesn't.

He embraces me.

We weep.

I offer him gifts of livestock.

He refuses.

I insist.

He accepts.

He wants to travel together.

I tell him to go ahead.

I'll be right behind him.

But, we part ways again

for I am a born-fighter.

I am a God-wrestler.

Prayer: How can we live at peace with You and wrestle with Your presence in our lives? How can we live at peace with one another as long as there is fear in our hearts? Lord, only through You can we overcome adversity and get along with others. May we give to one another, not out of fear, but out of a desire to set aside our differences. In the Prince of Peace, we pray, Amen.

Joy

Joseph, bowing low

Over Mary's shoulder, sees

Yahweh's Son's first smile.

While Bethlehem Sleeps

she nuzzles her face near His ear,

His milky breath sweet as honey warms

her heart as it fills with silent promises, and

His first earthly grip tightens on her hand.

His Mother's Joy

Did she realize in her wonderment,

as she played with her child's feet still wet
     just after birth,

held his tiny wrist and stroked the cushy center
     of his palm,

watched his round belly rise and fall,

laughed as she tickled his side,

believed that in him through his birth
     her joy was complete,

that one day

she would touch her child's feet still wet
     just after death,

hold his wounded wrist and stroke the cushy center
     of his palm,

watch his sunken belly still,

weep as she rubbed his pierced side,

believe that in him through his death
     her joy would be complete?

Gift

Gilded starry knot, rays wrapped across the sky

Incarnate child sleeping in the hay,

Father God conducting angelic chorus in surround

Tonight proclaim Messiah's first birthday.

While Bethlehem Sleeps

Old Simeon hears his heart

still

beating

on the day he holds

Incarnate God

beholds

the face

no one lives

after seeing

a light, a glory

that pierces souls

and hearts reveals.

On Watching a Church Choir
One Sunday

Notes glide from beneath bow on strings,

trombone slide ties the melody, trumpet bursts declare,

and well-known words slip from tongue tips,

yet no smiles, no eyes alight

only glares on glasses, vacant stares—

Where? Where! Where is joy on weary masks

creased with wrinkling cares

with mouths in motion yet no emotion,

and gazes down instead of

up. See! See with eyes closed to darkness, to despair.

Let lyrics lick wounds and repair the weeping soul.

Can you hear as I hear, see me with my love
     in the balcony,

his murmuring voice singing music he learned alone

while I knelt for years in prayer?

The Giver and the Gift[iv]

I broke my jar open,

Spilled nard over his feet,

Unbound my hair,

Wiped away the broken stone.

I broke my life open,

Spilled blood over my feet

Bound every sin,

Wiped away every broken heart.

Prayer: What joy we have in Christ! What joy when we can open our lives for Him to enter! With You, Lord, there is no fleeting happiness! Even in death, You gave us new life, making new vessels out of our broken lives! Keep us praising at Your feet! With overflowing joy, we pray, Amen.

Love

Little hands touch the nail

  in the wood of the manger;

Oval eyes stare at the star,

  the light from heaven;

Very acute ears listen

  beyond the brays of the animals;

Even the taste of his first meal

  does not seem to distract him.

Large hands hang on the nails

  in the wood of the cross

Oval eyes fill with tears,

  the sorrow of heaven;

Very acute ears listen

  beyond the shouts of the people;

Even the taste of bitter vinegar

  does not seem to distract him.

While Bethlehem Sleeps

Shekinah rests in a manger.

The Word breathes in and out.

Torah lives.

For a Moment

before shepherds peer inside the manger

crowds press in seeking healing,

pleading for signs, praising with palms

preventing her parental protection

before Magi gifts of gold, of fragrant

alabaster fragments fall

at the feet her fingers fondle,

those footprints with followers who flee,

her jumbled thoughts join with rapt joy,

impenetrable pulsating peace,

lavish love of and for her Lord.

These and heaven's hope, she harbors in her heart.

Snow

An Excerpt

Why do I love you?

Why do I need to live

where you fall

not just in inches, but in feet

so that my own sink

into your depths,

my boots becoming cups

for you to fill?

It's no more

than remembering

the thrill of sledding hills.

Snowflakes

Why does He bother to intricately design
        something that melts away?

Because He knows what they cannot know—

He remembers the pleasure of each creative snip;

He sees the holes the wind blows through
        their brief, lacy existence;

He calculates the distance they fall,
        makes sure they float and land softly.

And when the sun comes,
        its light warming their patterns away,

He gives them one last gift beyond their outer beauty—

He allows their evaporation to water sleeping seeds.

The Red Convertible

There was a boy

who loved his father's red convertible,

the one restored over years,

the one stored over seasons,

brought out only in sunny weather,

and driven only on side streets.

But, the boy would sneak it out,

not an easy task

with its boat-like size,

rumbling engine, and dark-cloud exhaust.

Once he rolled his own car

into the bumper, denting it,

and though he paid back in punishment

there was joy in owning a piece

of the car he hoped to inherit one day,

so convinced was he of its value.

Then one Christmas it was given,

the deed signed over.

The boy felt joy and gratitude,

for now he owned it all,

not realizing possession of his father's treasure

would mean maintaining it

with a new carburetor, spark plugs,

touch-up paint, shocks,

soon discovering it provided conditional pleasure

because it could only be enjoyed
            when weather permitted.

Suddenly, it became just a something

taking up space in the garage.

There was joy in selling it

to someone who would love it again,

and renewed conviction in building

a different, personal dream

to fill that space with something else,

something his sons could hope to inherit,

something that could certainly be memorable

for the pleasure it could bring,

and more importantly,

something his father never owned:

a red boat.

Warmed Memories

On New Year's Eve,

Mom takes the family calendar from its nail;

our family of five flips through the months,

then Mom tears each page from the spiral

throws it into the flames.

We watch the paper curl and char.

Such a violent way

to end and begin a year?

Some memories, the hot ones,

I want turned to cinders.

But some pages spark their own fires,

warming my back on my coldest days.

Father and Son[v]

I walked into our family garden

carrying a loaf of fresh-baked bread

and a trophy-sized fish caught that morning.

I couldn't wait to share them with my son.

After I called for him, he ran to me instantly,

the way the sheep come when I enter the fields.

As I held out my gifts to him,

I noticed he held two things himself:

a jagged stone and a garden snake.

"Why do you have these things in your hands?" I asked.

"They are not for you, Father," he said in a sullen tone.

"My brother threw a stone at me this morning,
      so this one is for him.

This snake is for my sister's bed."

"I see," I said, motioning for him to sit next to me.

"Do you remember what you asked me yesterday?

You said you looked for me all day.

You almost knocked me down
          when we met in the fields."

"I asked you if we could spend some time together,"
          he replied.

"Then why are these things in your hands?"

He answered by dropping the stone in the dust.

We ate our lunch,

watching the snake slither away in the grass.

Prayer: Lord, we praise You for the Father You are to us. You give us daily what we need. You prove Your unconditional love by Your tender gifts, by Your desire to spend time with us. May we give to one another as You give. Remind us we cannot love You fully without fully loving one another. In Your loving Name, we pray, Amen.

Faith

Fill my veins with blood reborn;

Alter the DNA of my sinner's soul;

Infuse belief, like placental

Transfer, nurturing

Hope with the conception of new life.

While Bethlehem Sleeps

an Eastern Magi studies his star charts

once, twice, three times.

The beacon traveling west

appears nowhere

on the known maps

outshines the fixated guide star.

As he marks its course,

counts his gifts,

it beckons him to step

on an untraveled path.

Make Us Wisdom Walkers,

following Your will's star as we travel life's desert.

May we be as those first gifts:

precious gold, refined by Your Spirit's fire;

incense, our prayers a fragrant smoke
        before Your presence;

myrrh, pain-relieving balm for
        your royal priesthood, the Body.

But, Lord, before we reach You, as we seek Your face,

may we give the Child what He desires most—
        our hearts, our souls, our minds.

The Followers

We, the Followers,

among the sheep

of the Shepherd

who are counted

in the census

of the Kingdom,

hear beyond angels' songs

the Newborn's cry,

journey through deserts

under the Star,

passing wise men,

longing to see the Lamb

face to face.

Follow the Star

I wish myself a shepherd as I lead my little ones along,

warning them about bramble-bush choices,

guiding them to peaceful streams and nourishing
    earth food,

watching over them as they play in the meadows,

smiling over their little heads as they breathe deep
    in the night.

I wish myself a wise one as I teach them all I know,

searching for knowledge and truth from God's Word,

studying those He has provided with prose and insight,

enjoying the creation and marveling at its variety,

giving back through my gifts of labor and love.

I wish myself a sheep as I seek the Lord each day,

looking for His Morning Star to guide me,

traveling with my wise man through deserts
    and up mountains,

coaxing our lambs along the righteous path,

glorifying and praising our loving Shepherd
    while journeying this life.

How Is It a Lamb?

How is it a lamb

calls sheep,

these shepherds listening

to angels' songs about this newborn

lying in a feeding trough?

How is it a lamb

saves sheep

who follow him to sacrifice

their blemished skin spared,

his perfect wool stained red?

Somehow it is this lamb

who loves sheep

enough to die for them,

to rise above their stubborn hearts,

to become their shepherd's voice.

The King and the Queen^{vi}

I had to see it for myself.

I had to see this great King Solomon from the north.

His palace was grander than I imagined.

No one described it in its full splendor.

I asked him every hard question on my mind.

He answered every one!

As we talked together, I could see why

The people in his kingdom are so happy.

I understood this man could only be wise

Because of his loving, righteous God.

I could not hold back my praise

For a God who would give like this.

I gave my gold and precious stones freely.

My spices filled Solomon's storage houses.

In turn, he gave me riches from his holdings,

Promising to give me my greatest desire.

All I had desired was a trade agreement.

I never dreamed I would make a friend.

Prayer: Thank you for showing Your glory in the great gifts You give us. When others see what You have done in our lives, may it encourage them to believe in You. When it is difficult to see Your hand in a situation, may it only strengthen and renew our faith. In Your faithful Name, we pray, Amen.

Make Me Believe in Christmas

for Clifford A. Olson (1909-1978)

and

for Nate and all children who seek the truth

"Is there such a thing as Santa?"

my child asked on his eighth Christmas,

with the same indignant scowl

he gave when he received

a present wrapped in the same paper

I used to wrap his teacher's gift.

Not knowing how to answer for a legend

I'd never really told,

but had never denied,

or ever believed myself

since discovering my own gifts

on shelves, unwrapped, at age four,

I told him a story...

A little boy, who was not quite old enough to know he was poor because he still survived on dreams, went to see Santa at the mall. Sitting on the edge of the bearded man's knee, he shared his secret wishes not even his father knew. But, wanting to know more about the man inside the red coat, he left his mother, pushed apart a curtain, and entered a forbidden place where a clean-shaven man in a T-shirt and Santa's pants yelled, "Get out!"

The startled boy backed away into the white-cuffed, red-velvet arms of his Santa, who looked at him with tender blue eyes like his own, picked him up with carpenter-worked hands like his father's, and carried him to his mother who gave Santa a kiss on the cheek before they left for home.

"The little boy was my father,

and the Santa was his father,"

I said with a telling smile.

And in that moment

my child believed in Christmas

without the make-believe.

To the Stocking Stuffer

On this morn of dawning surprises,

take my life,

like a stocking

hanging on the mantle of Your grace,

fill it with

hope for all things new;

joy for many sufferings;

peace of mind for decisions;

and unconditional love for the world

saved through the True Gift of this hour;

then bless it with faith like a child's

during the coming year.

While Bethlehem Sleeps

restlessly through blasting bombs

casting shadows on mass tombs,

one cave,

a short-lived grave,

remains

a vacant room

for leaders gone astray

for the wise seeking another way

for the faithful knowing to stay

for those dying for the day

the blasting horn

awakens the reborn.

Answer Our Heart Cry, O Child of the Star!

Guide us to Your manger, container of our Daily Bread.

Illuminate our inner caves with the pure truth
of Your call.

Lead us from our shrouded tombs and into
new morning glow.

Shine through us to reflect the miracle of rebirth.

The Spirit of New Names[vii]

Hear me all you in the churches!

Listen up!

For my sheep hear my voice.

They come when I call.

Follow me!

Be fishers of men!

Why do you wrestle with me in the night

When you have always had the birthright?

What is your heart's desire?

Just ask and it is yours!

Every unclean part of you

I will cleanse and make it whole.

Your prayers are like perfume to me.

Your life is this Potter's pride and joy.

There are so many things I want to give you.

There are so many ways you can serve me.

I have chosen each of you for a special purpose.

But, why won't you work together?

Not one of you is more important than the other.

You are all wanted, needed, and loved.

One day you will stand before me.

You will each receive a white stone.

It is your new name.

Only you and I know it.

You may have struggled in this world,

but through me you have overcome.

Do you hear me, my children?

Keep your ears wide open!

Prayer: Holy Spirit, fill us today with renewed purpose. May we use the gifts You have given us to work together. May others see us and want to join in serving You. Open our ears that we may hear Your constant call! As You lead us into this New Year, may we follow only You. In the name of our Gentle Shepherd, we pray, Amen.

Endnotes

[i] Based on 2 Kings 5; Ezekiel 11:19

[ii] Luke 2:14 NASB

[iii] Based on Genesis 32-33

[iv] Based on Matthew 26:7-13

[v] Based on Matthew 7:9-11

[vi] Based on 1 Kings 10:1-13

[vii] Based on Revelation 2:17; John 10:28; Mark 1:17; Genesis 32-33; 1 Kings 10:1-13; 2 Kings 5; Matthew 26:7-13; 1 Corinthians 12

6379624R00039